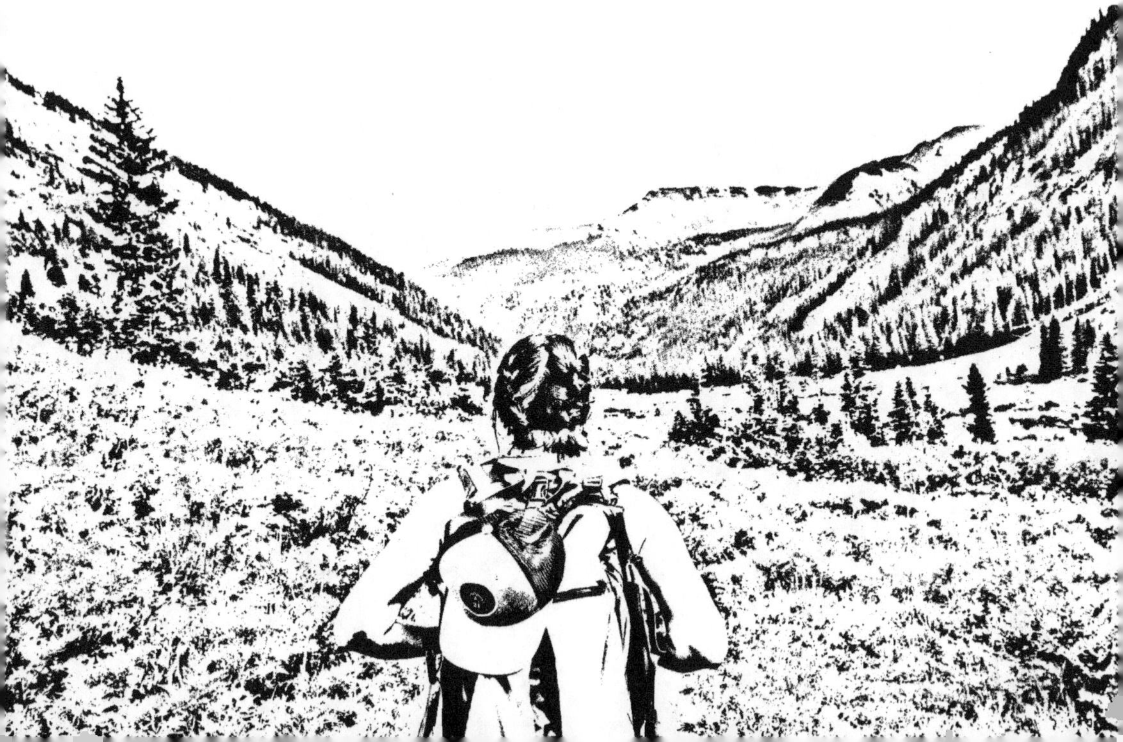

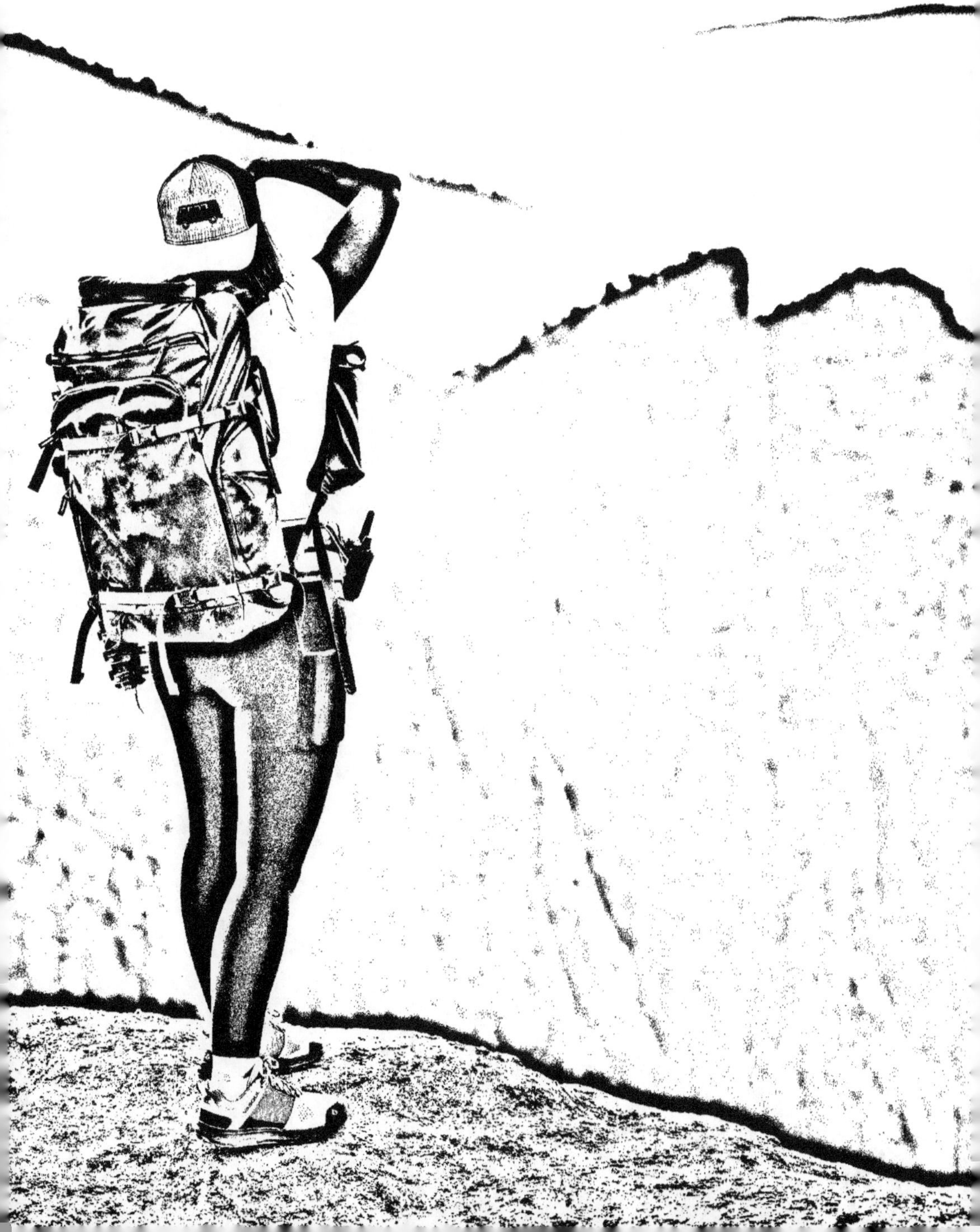

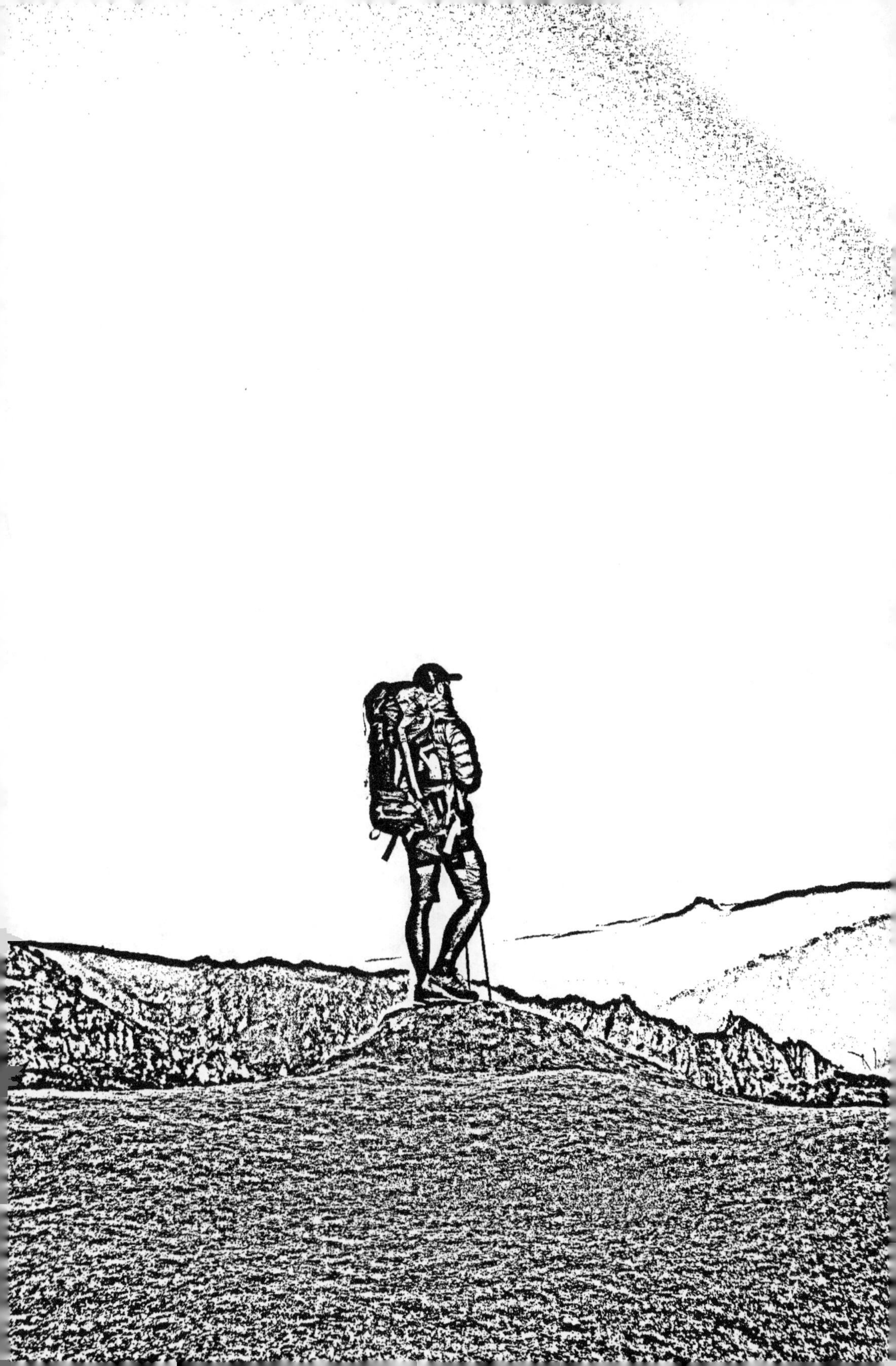

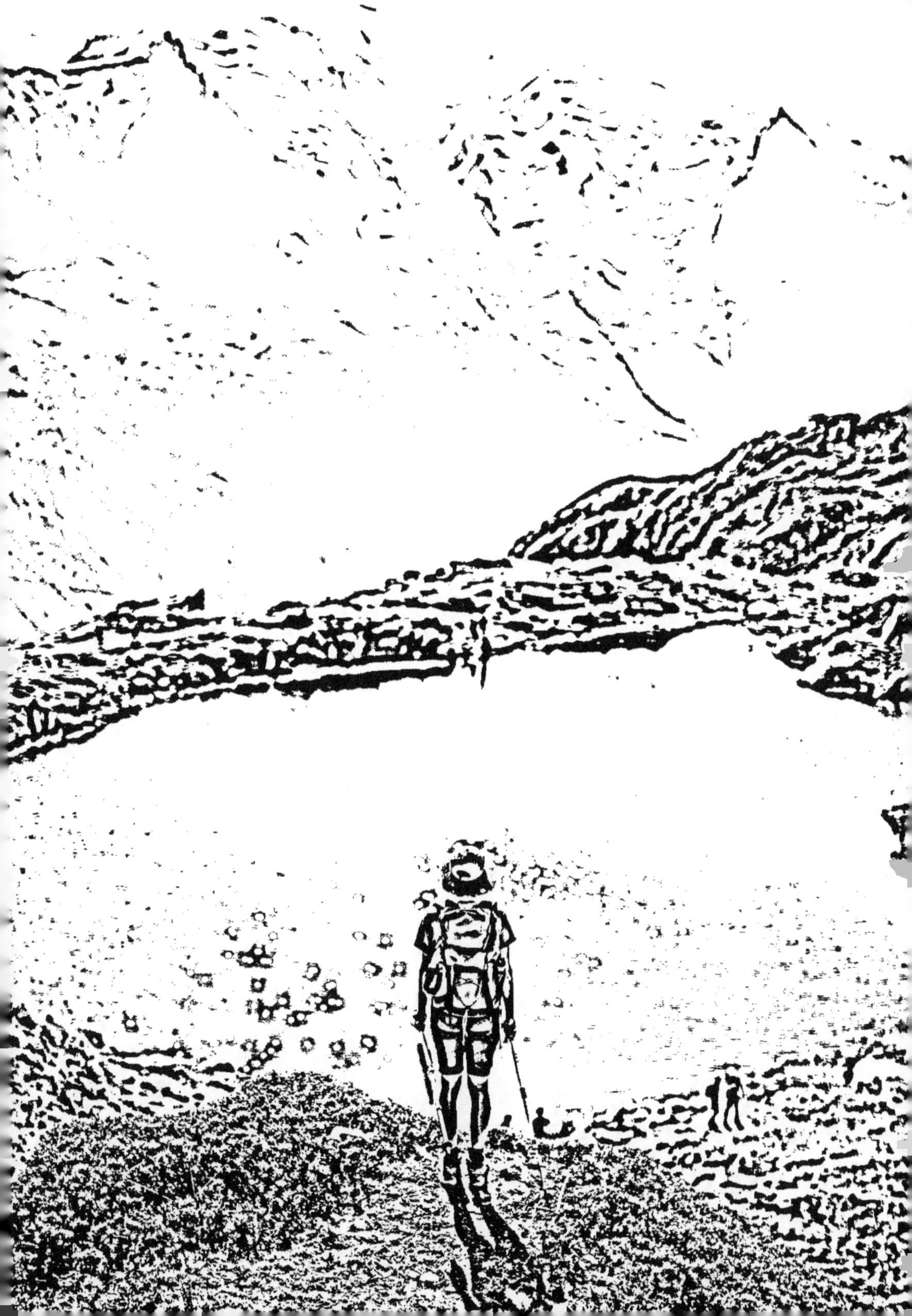

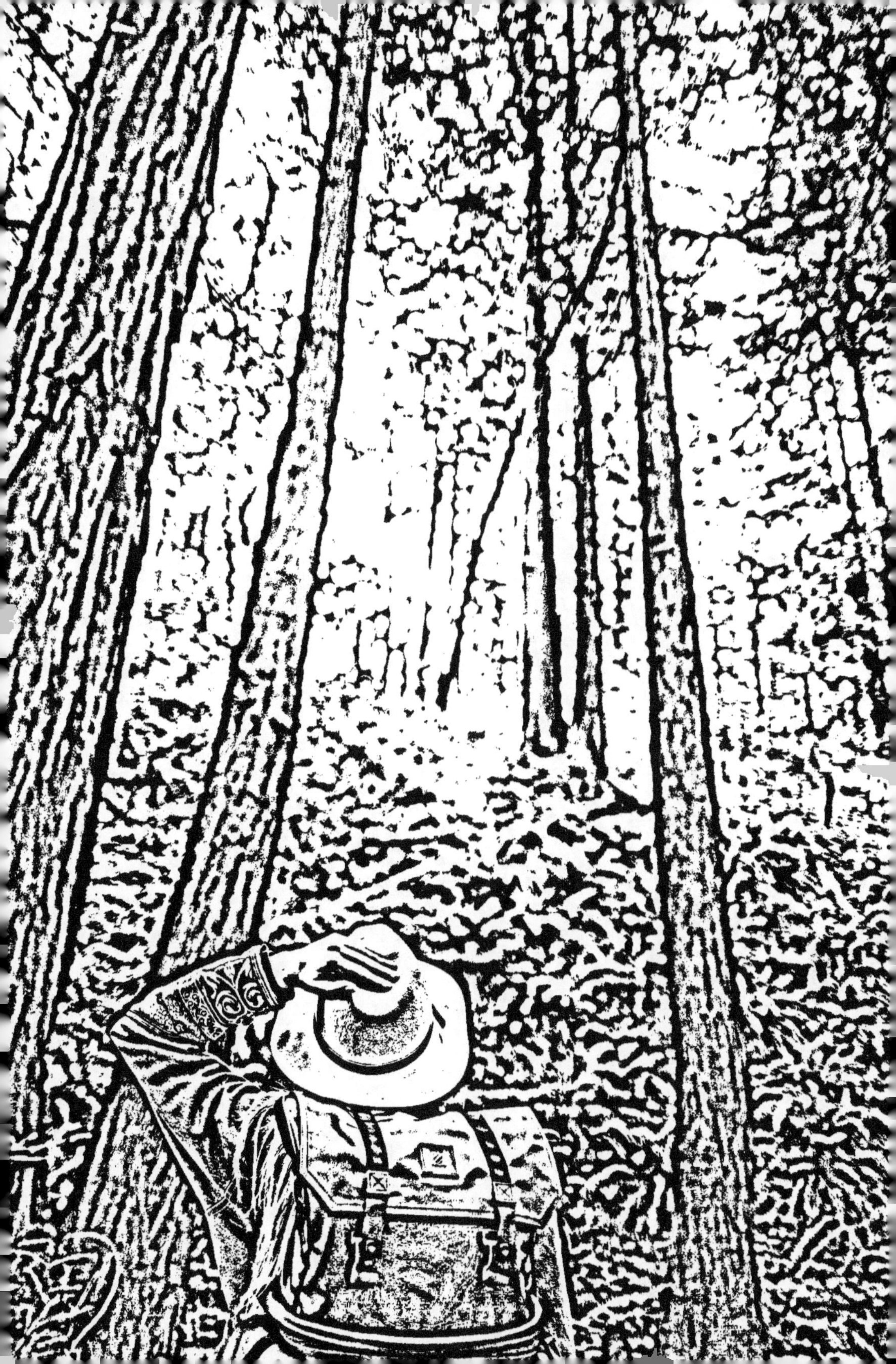

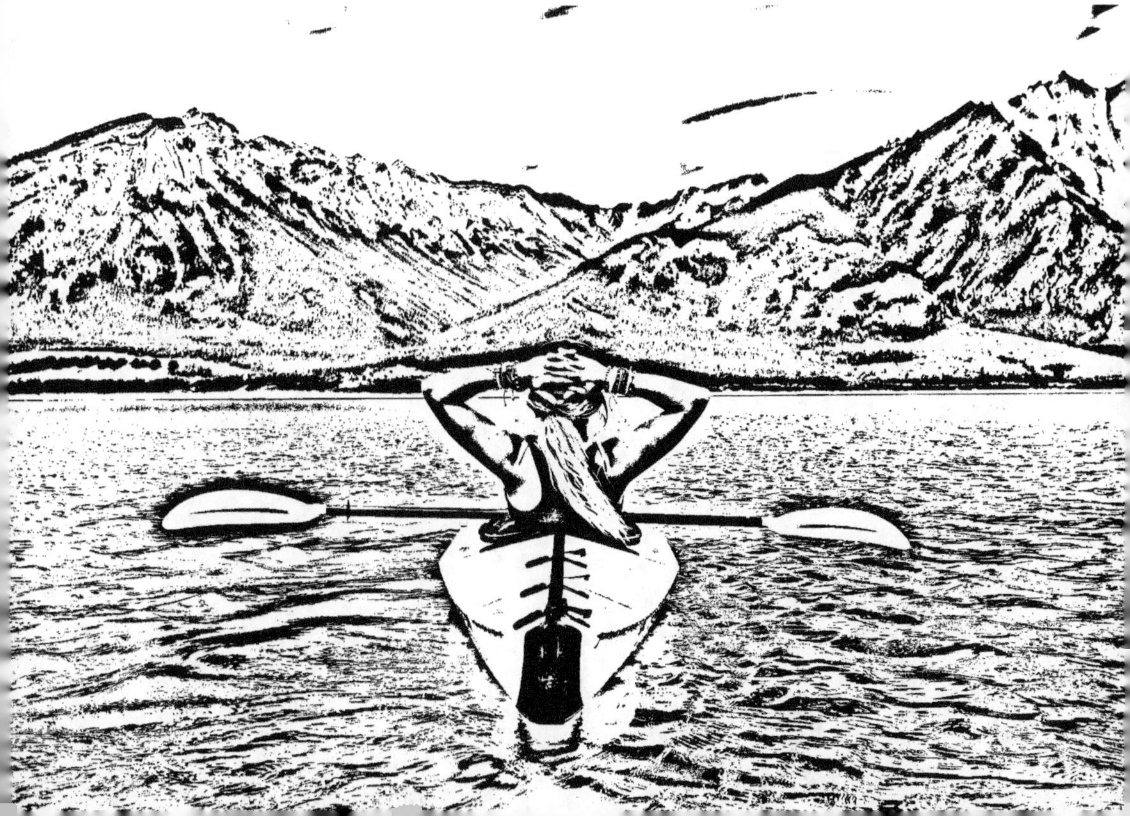

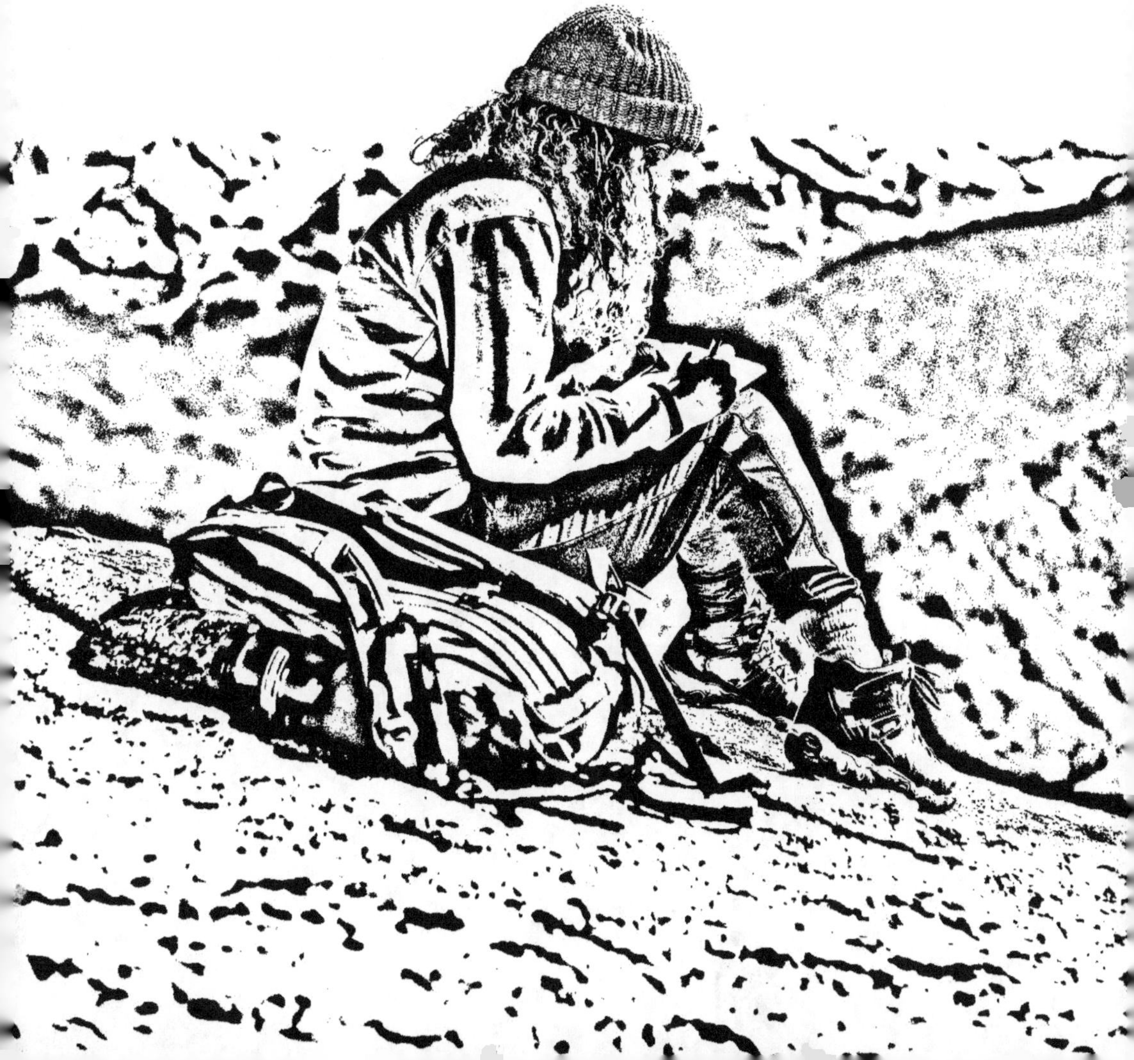

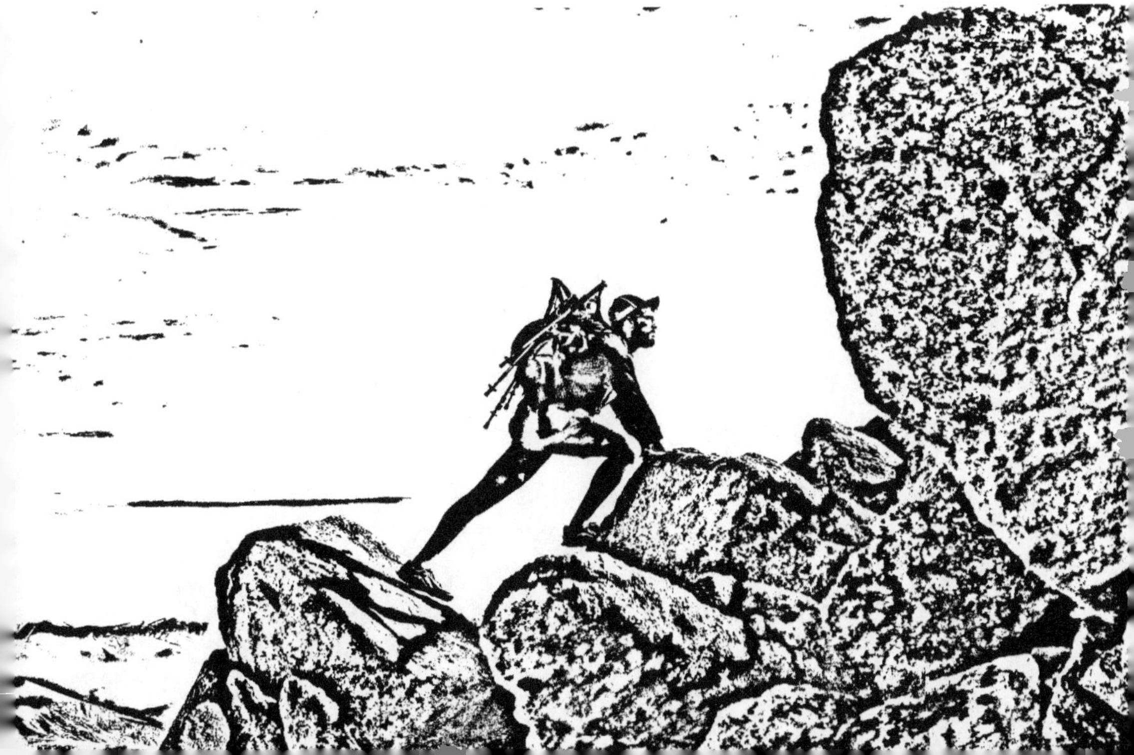

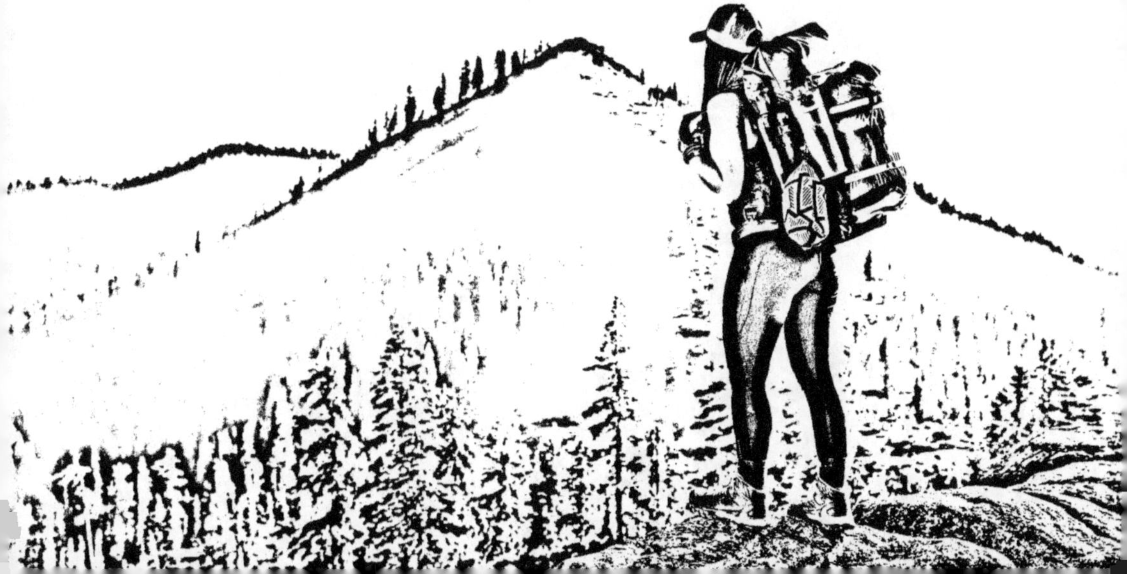

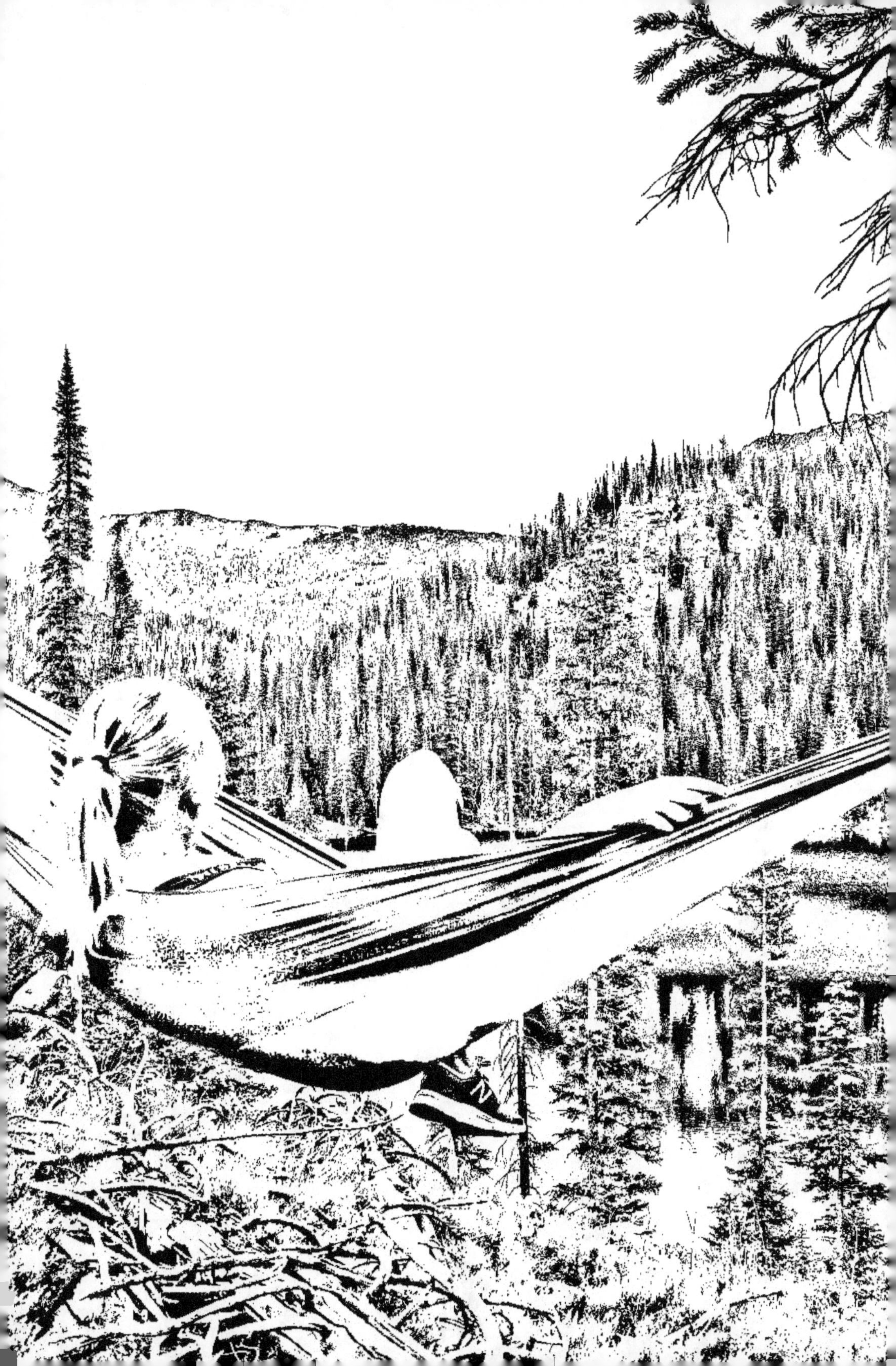

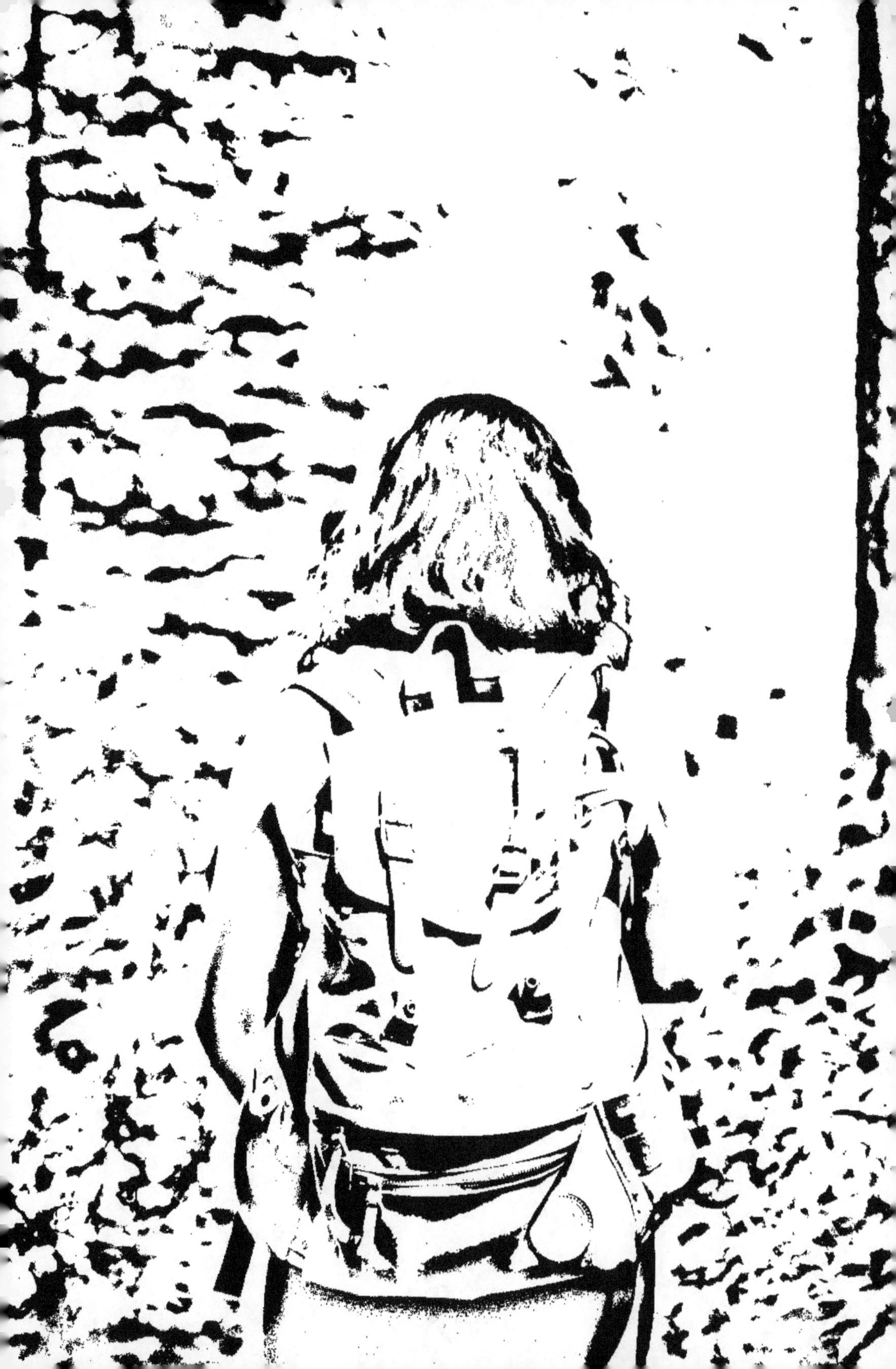

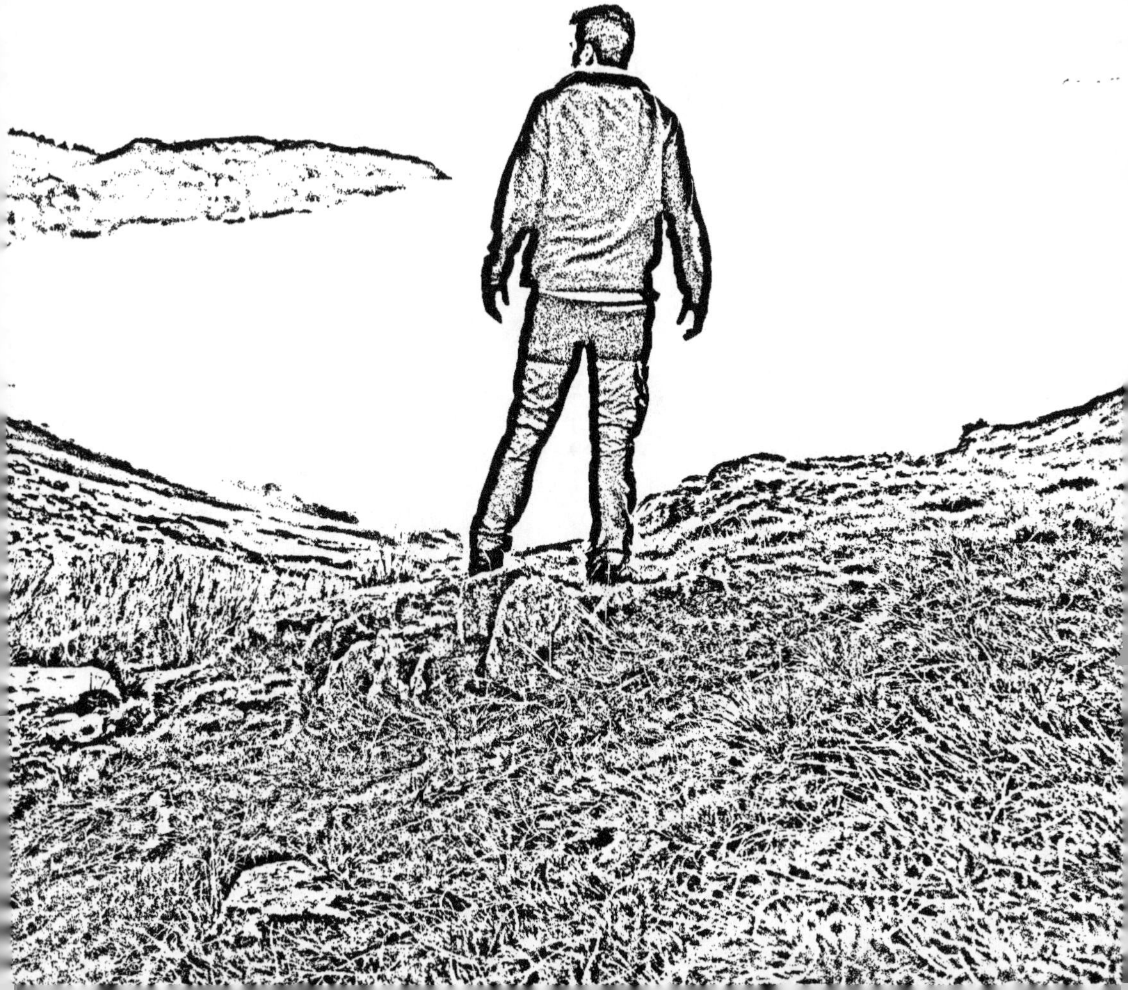

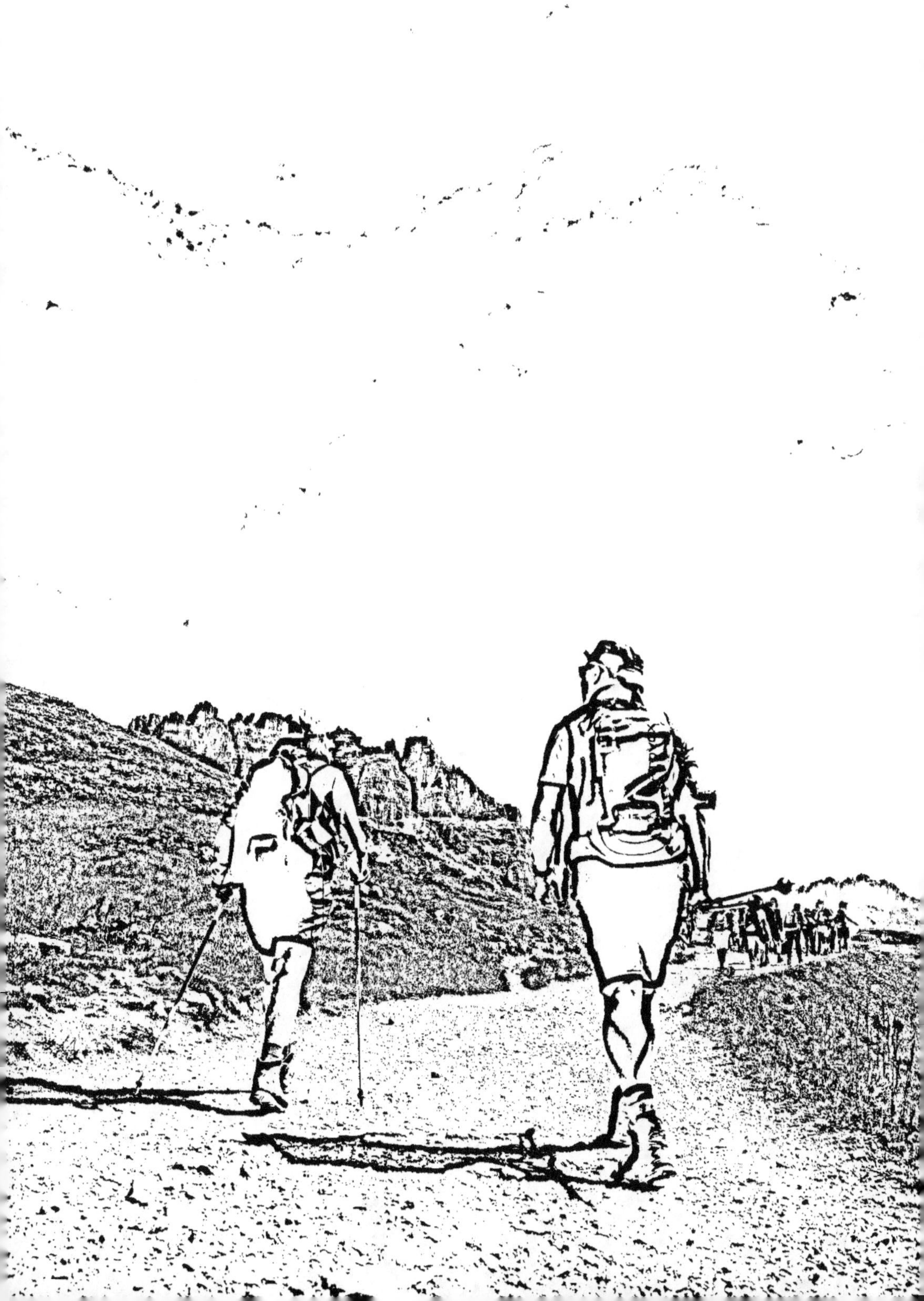

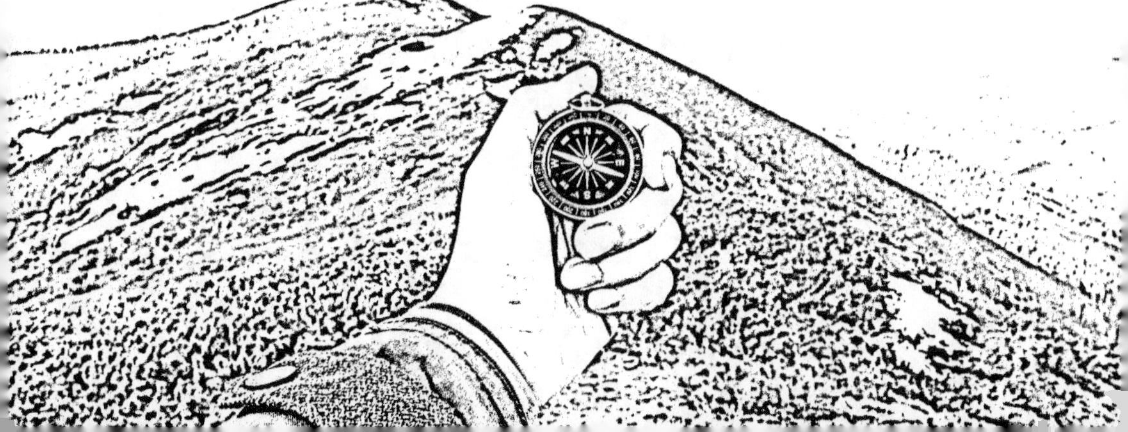

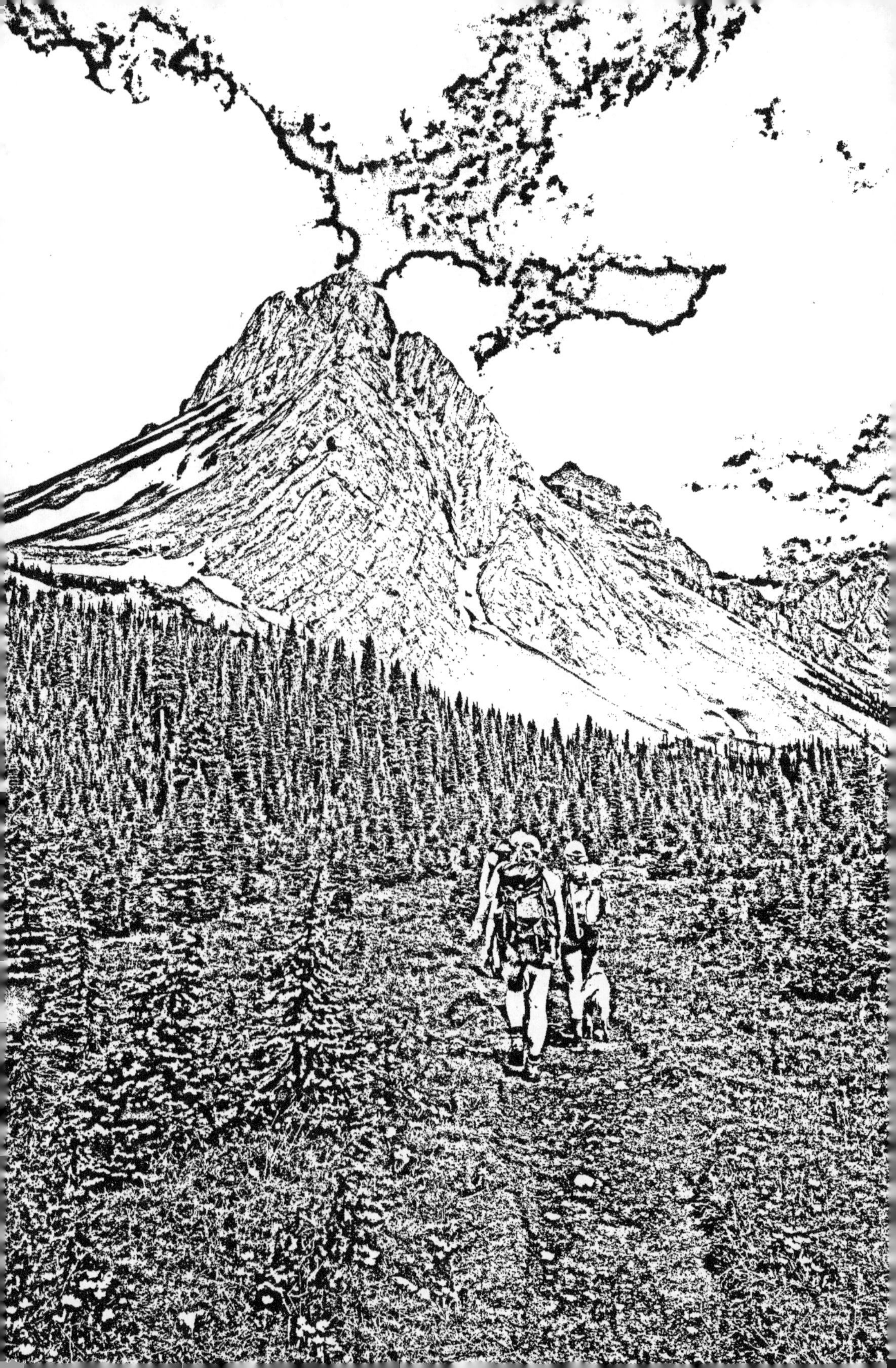

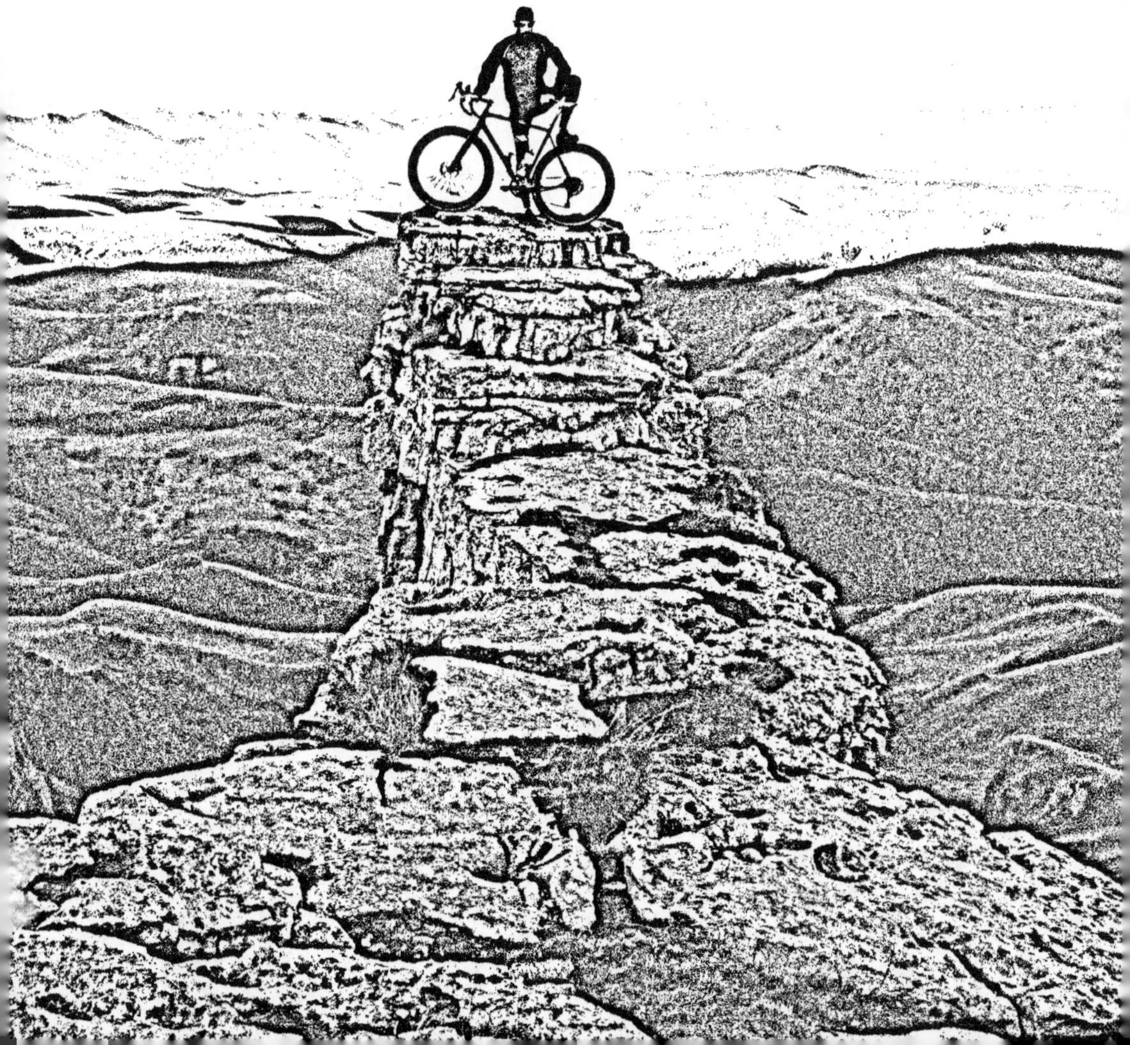

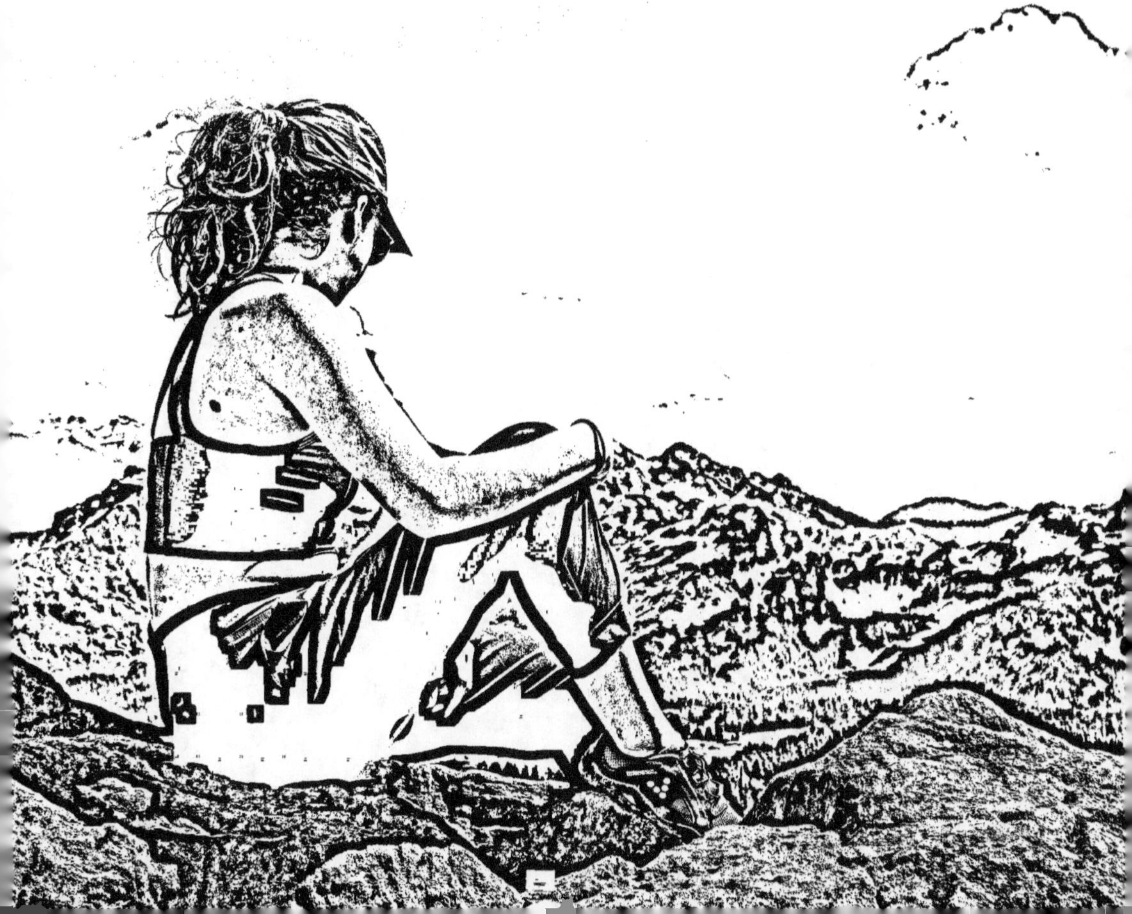

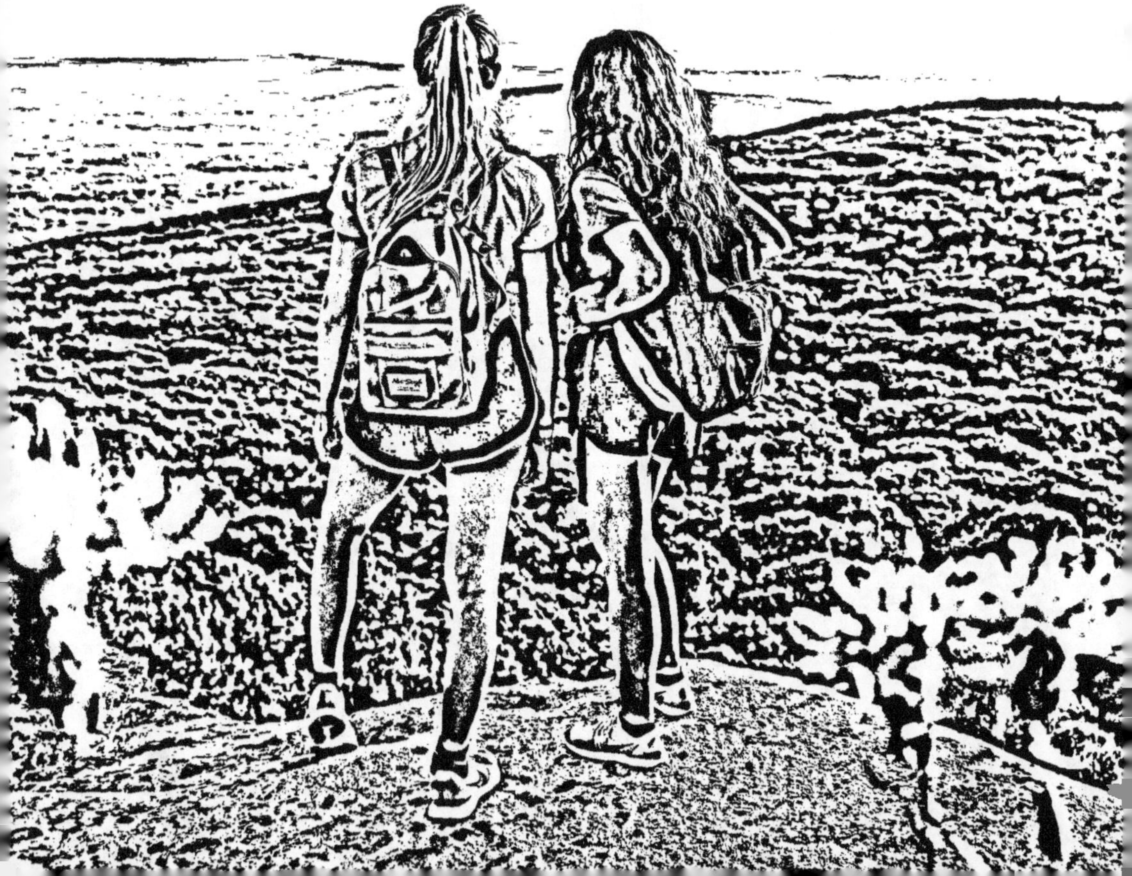

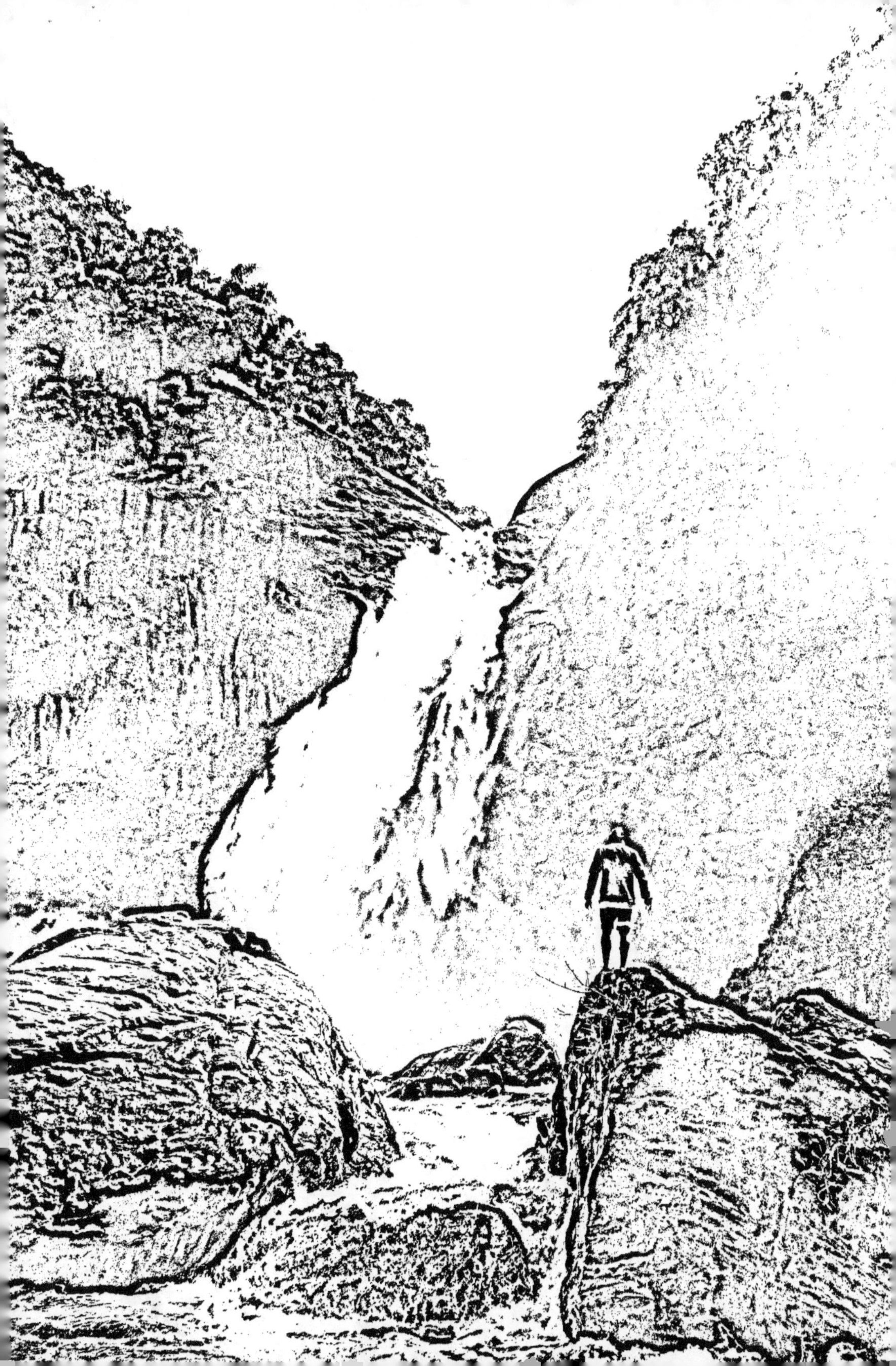

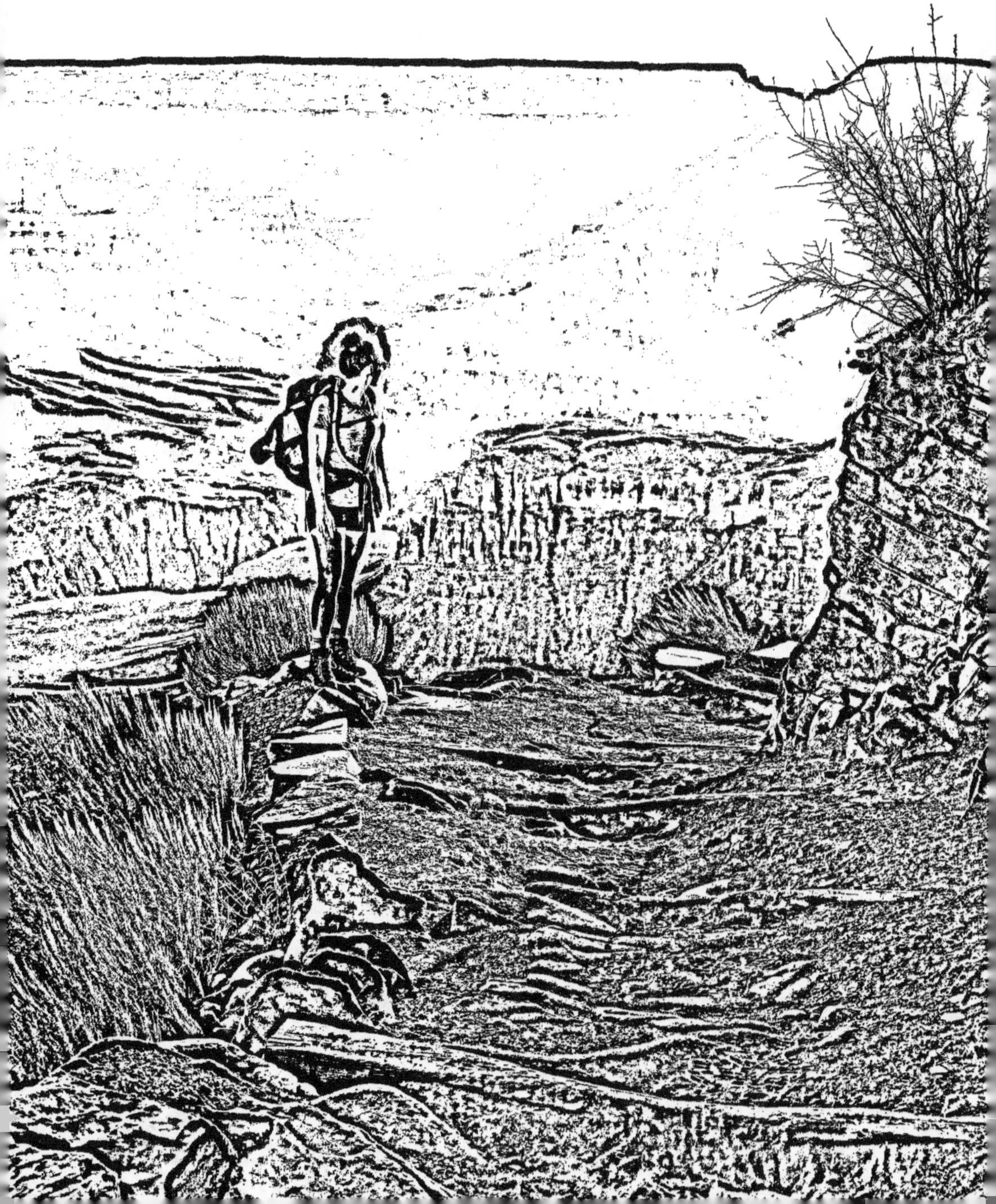

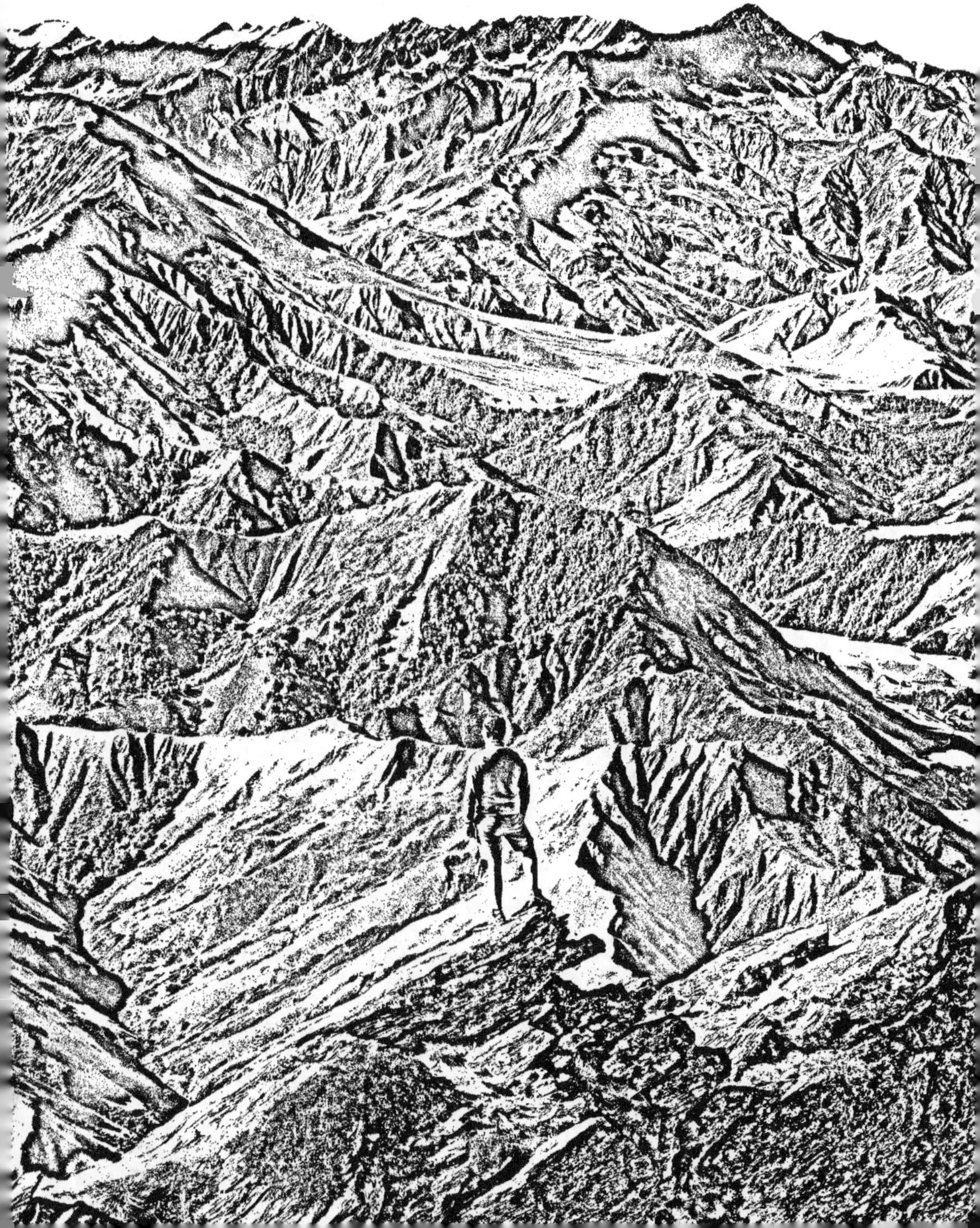

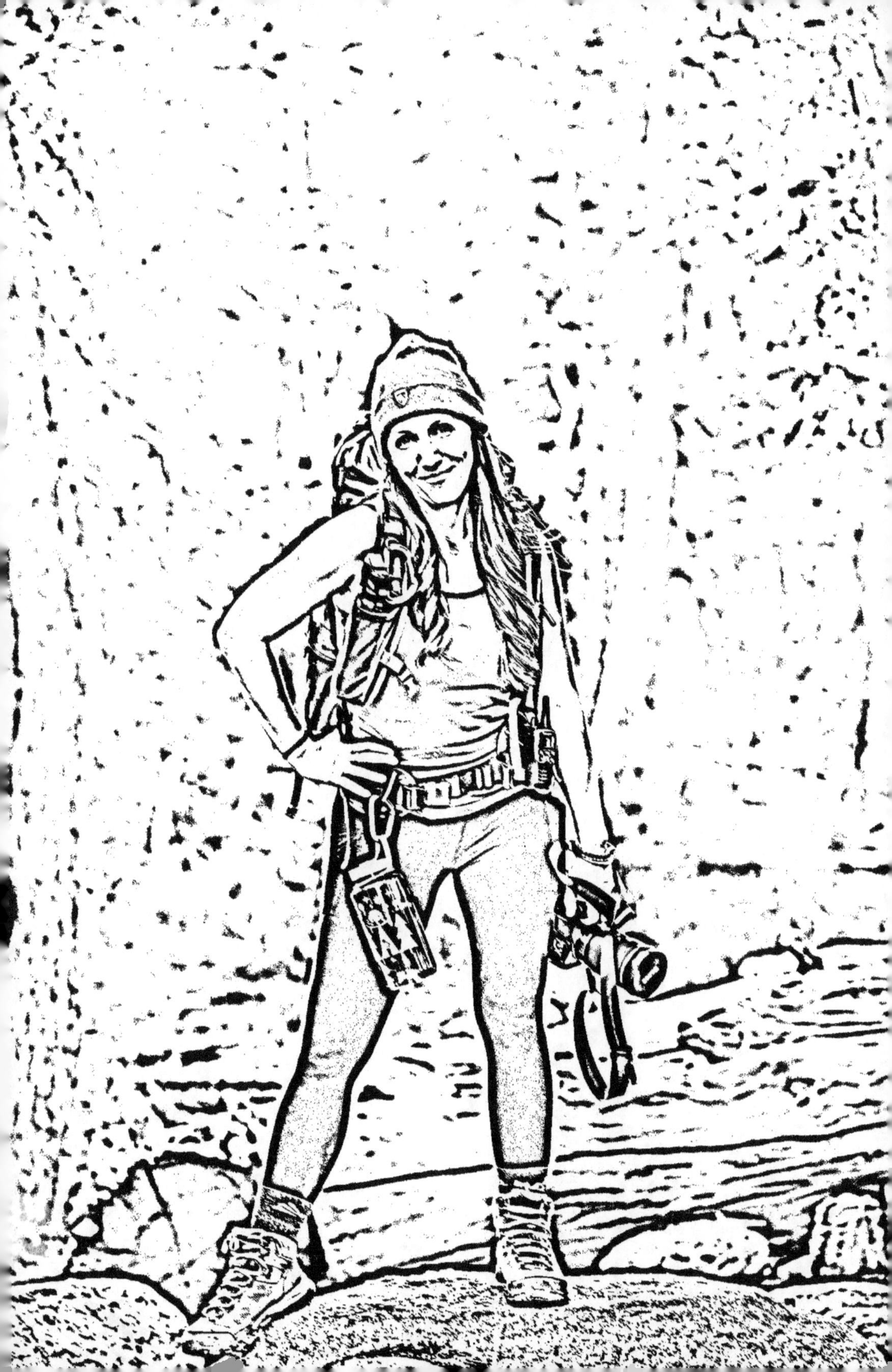

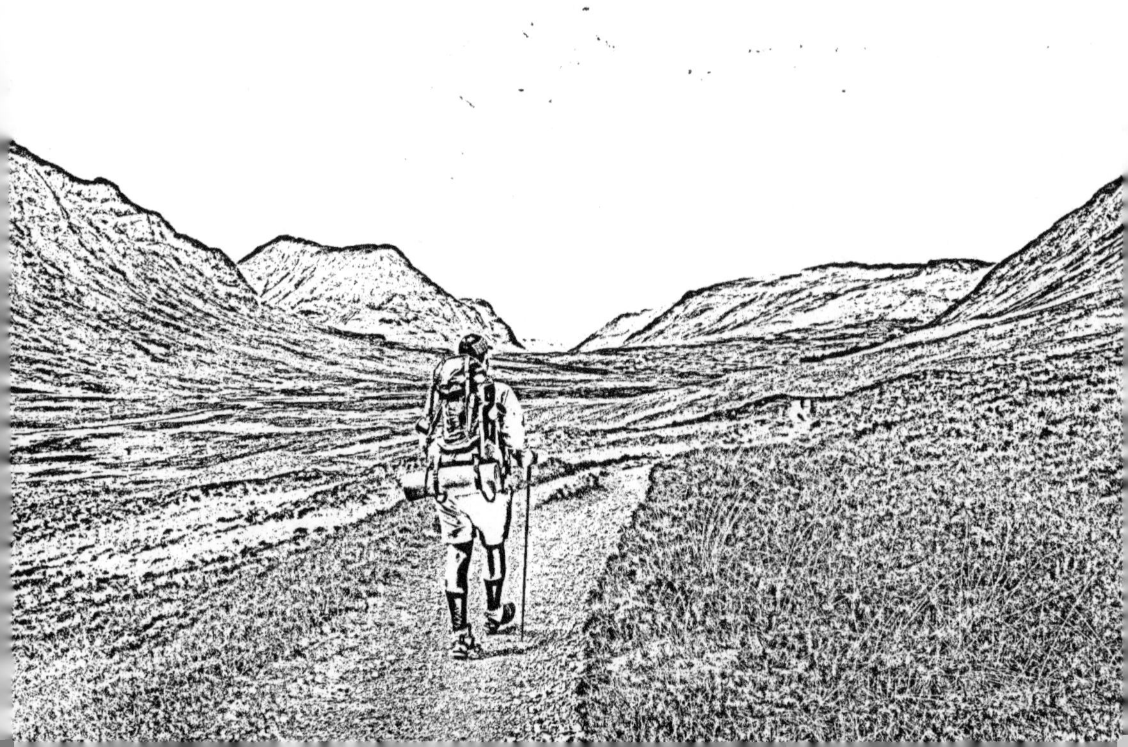

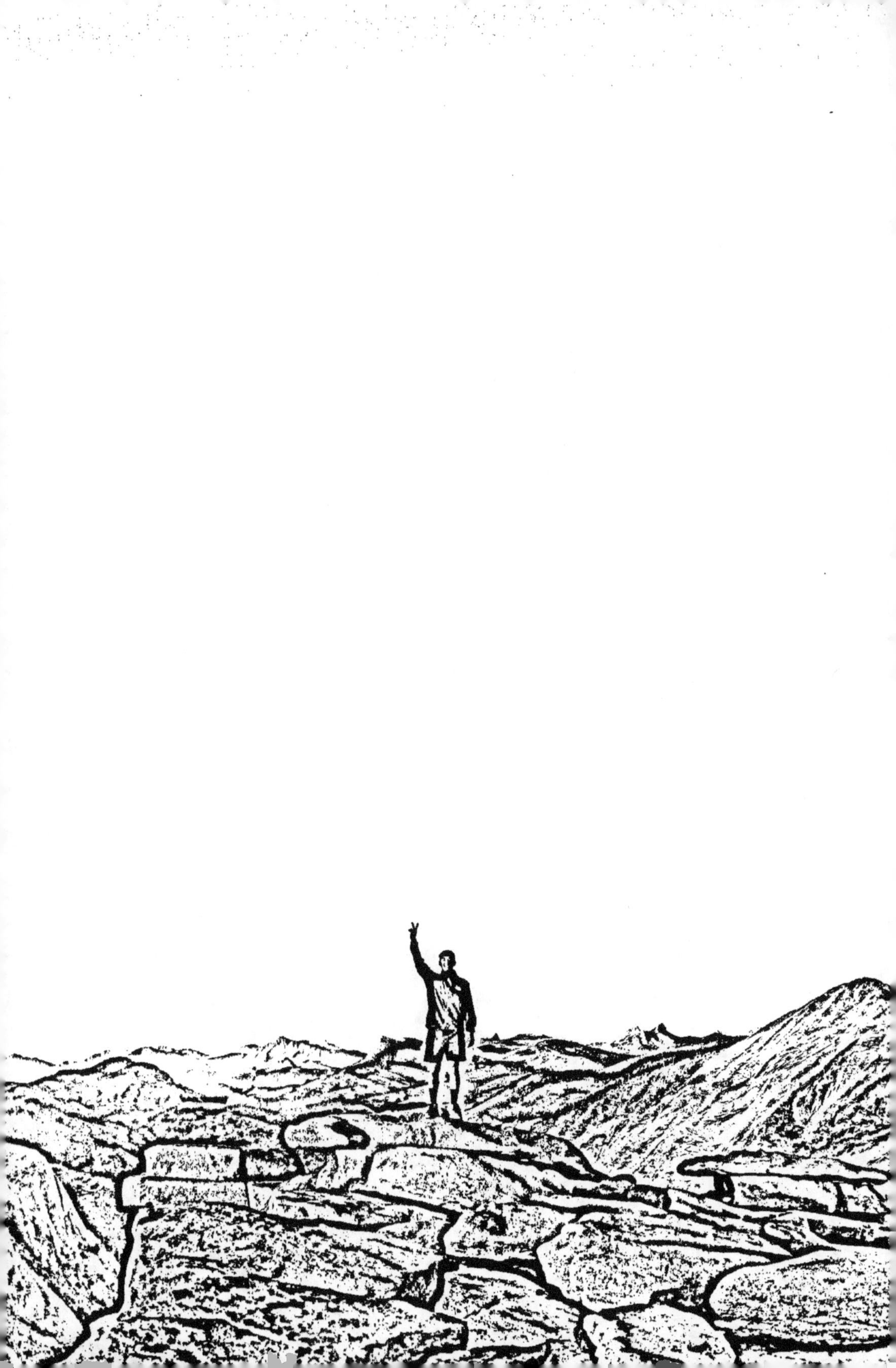

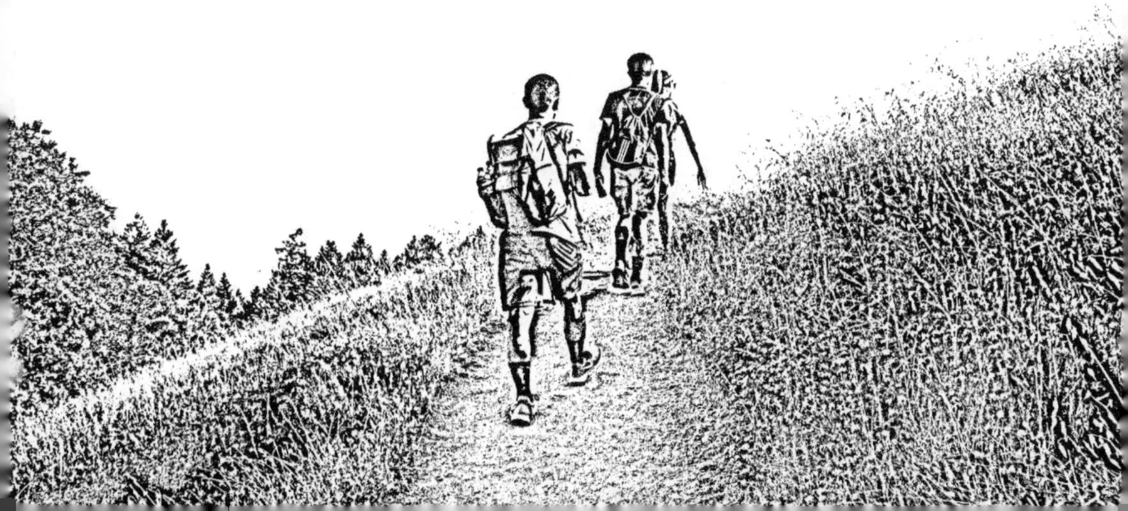

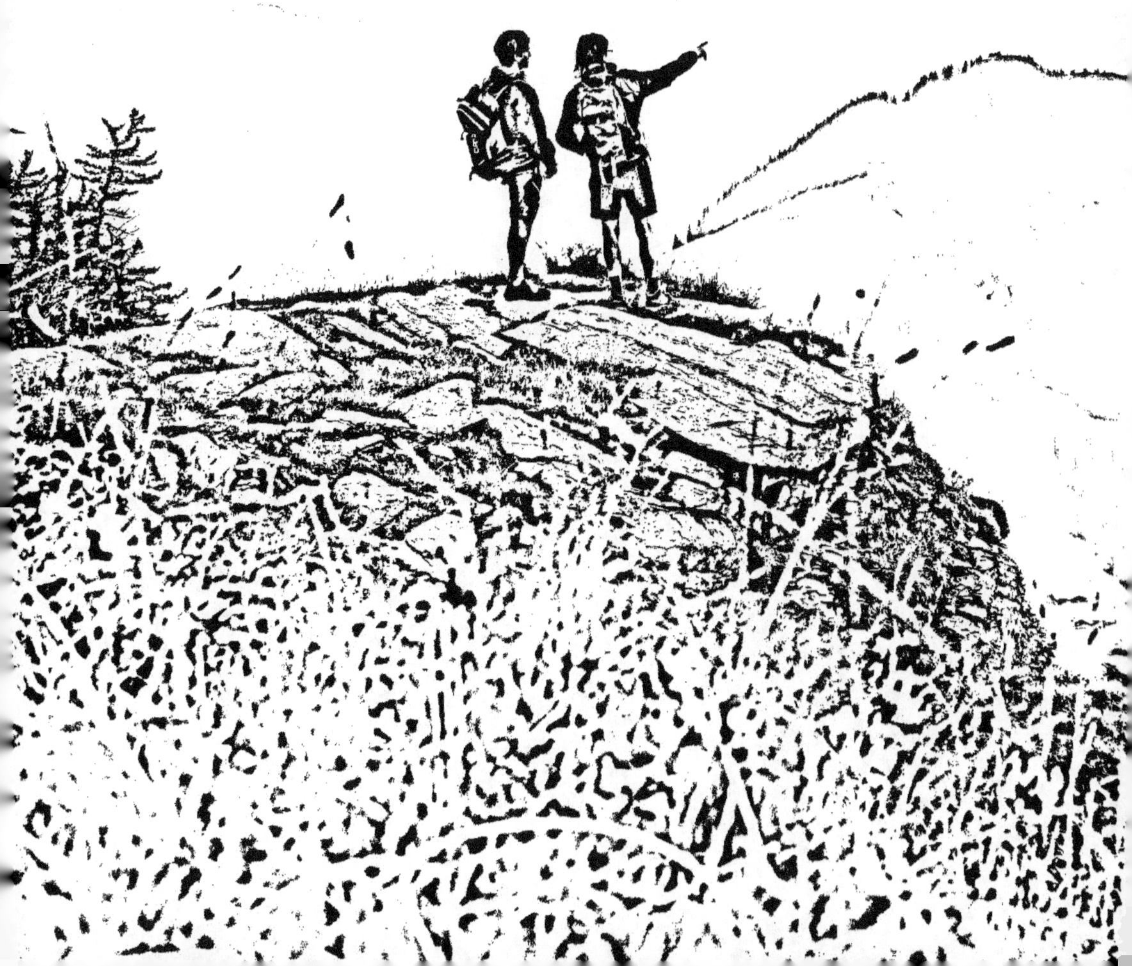

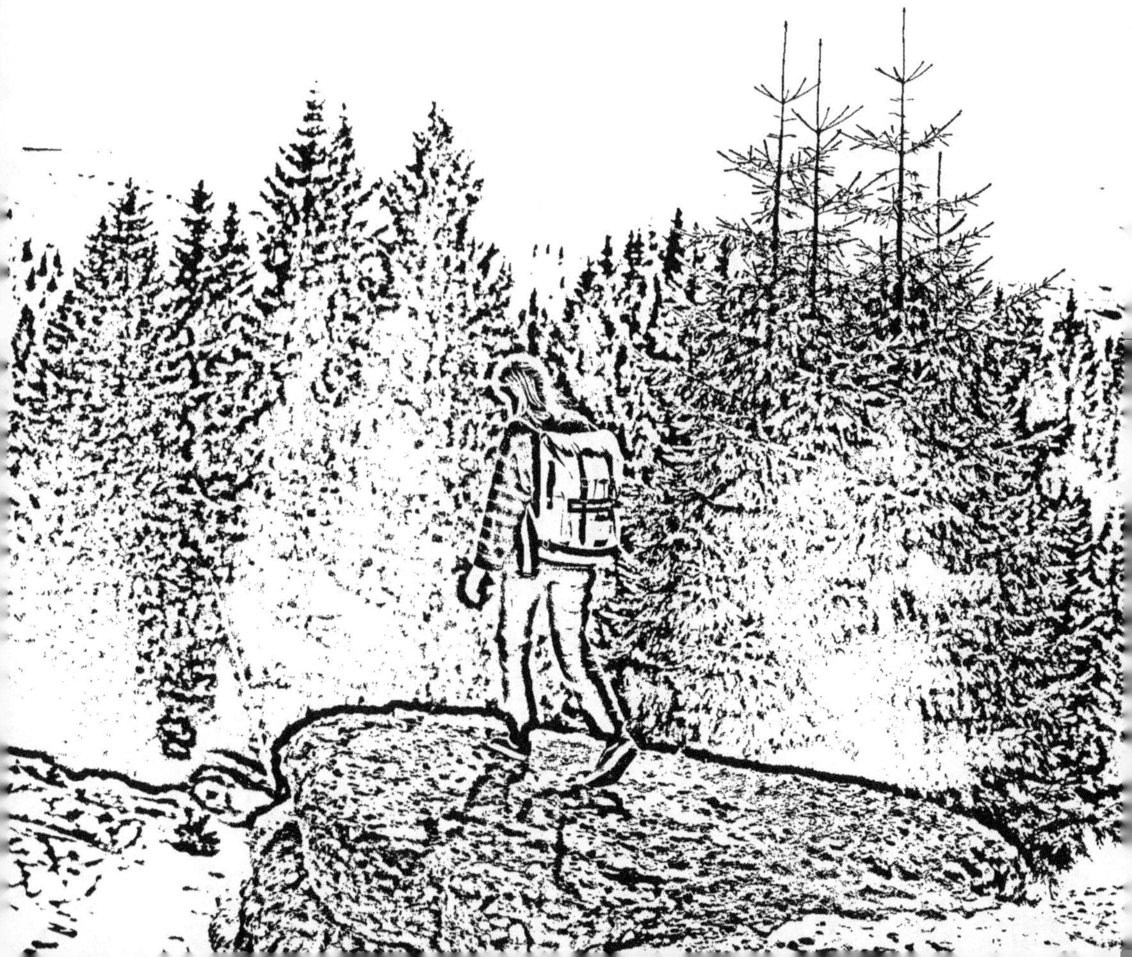

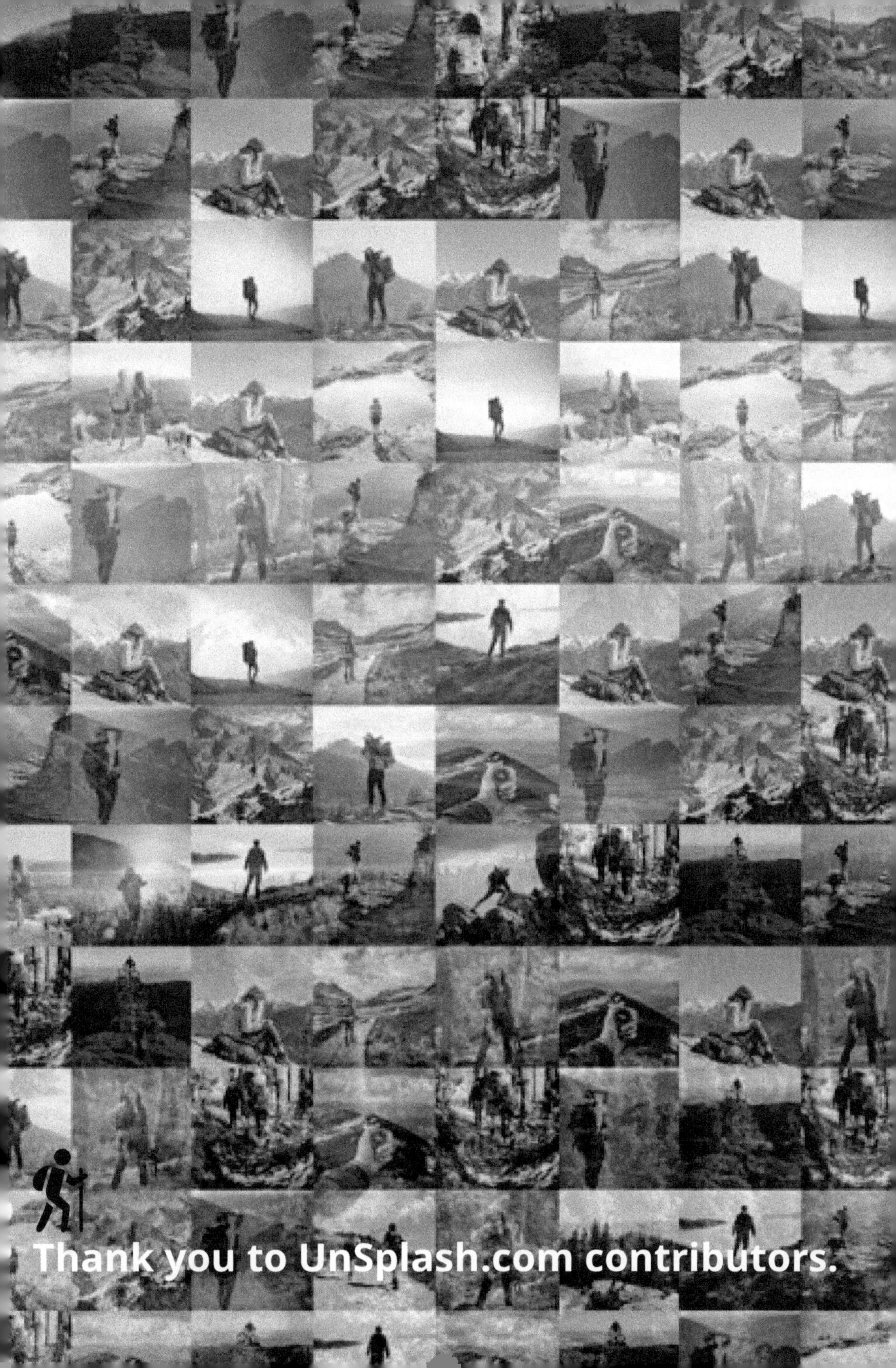
Thank you to UnSplash.com contributors.